# Color Me Musical
## Adagio Piano Book One

CMM Adagio
**1**
Piano Book 1

# Color Me MUSICAL

by Connie Cullum

# Color Me Musical:  Adagio Level
# Piano Book 1

Copyright ©2020 by Music Mentory

## MusicMentory.com

# Music Mentory Levels

### Color Me Musical
(Beginners ages 3 - 8)

Adagio
Moderato

### Bronze Beginners
(Beginners ages 9 - adult)

Adagio
Moderato

### Bronze

Allegro
Presto

### Silver

Adagio
Moderato
Allegro
Presto

### Gold

Adagio
Moderato
Allegro
Presto

### Platinum Virtuoso

Several fields of study available:

Teaching      Music Education      Performance      Composition

# Table of Contents

# This is a Dragon's Cave

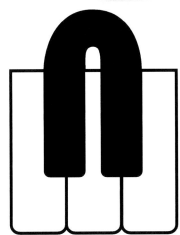

This is what it looks like
on the piano keyboard.

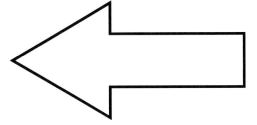

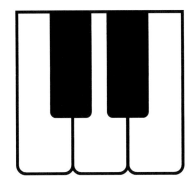

If you take the top off, you can
see that it is the **"two black key
group"** on the piano.

This is David.  He is a
Dragon.  He is **Purple**.

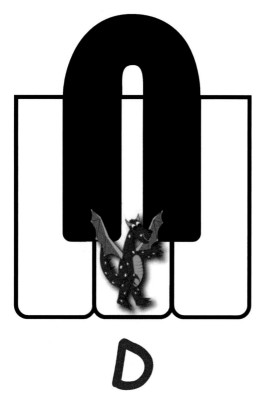

D

David lives
inside his
Dragon Cave
on the piano
keys.

# Play David the Dragon on the piano with your *Right Hand Pointer Finger*

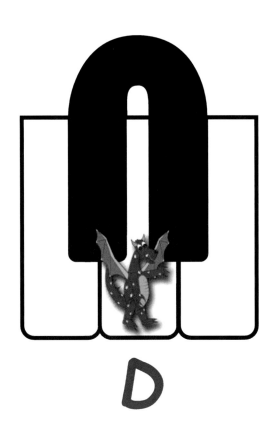

D

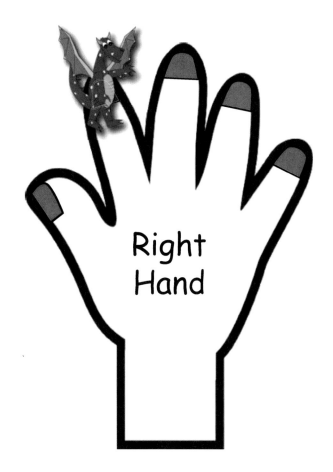

Right
Hand

# David the Dragon

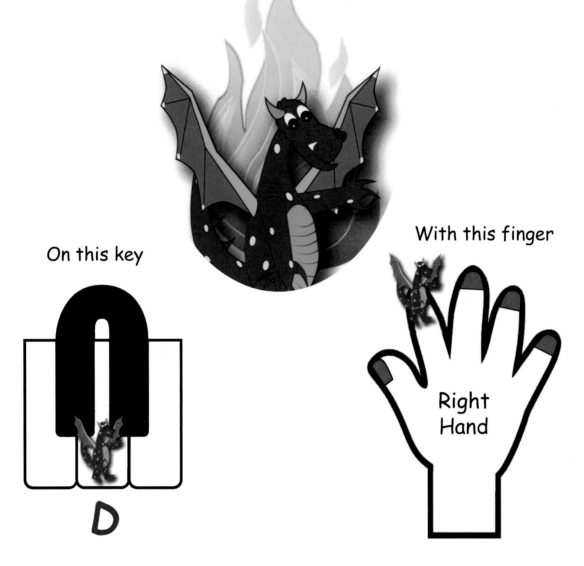

On this key

D

With this finger

Right Hand

Play: Say Dave's name every time you play his key on the piano.

Dave   Dave   Dave   Dave      Dave   Dave   Dave   Dave

# David the Dragon and the Rest

This is a REST.

When you see it, don't play a note.
Turn your palm up for one count.
Say "Rest" on that count.

Dave    Dave    Dave    Rest      Dave    Dave    Dave    Rest

# Rest, David, Rest

Play:

# The Resting Dragon

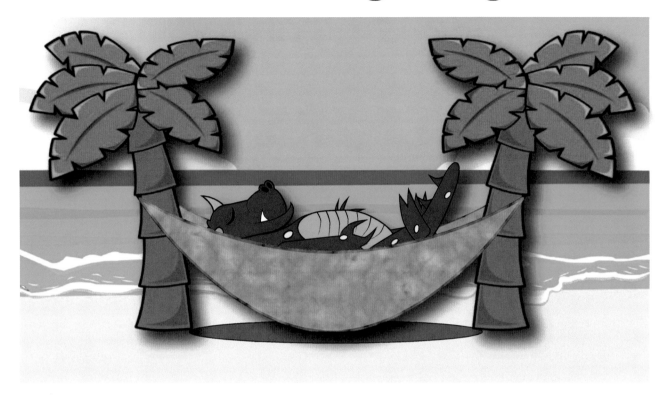

Play:

# This is Cade.  He is a Creature. He is Orange.

C

Cade is David's friend. He lives next to the Dragon's Cave.

Can you find where Cade lives on the piano?

# Cade the Creature

On this key

C

With your thumb

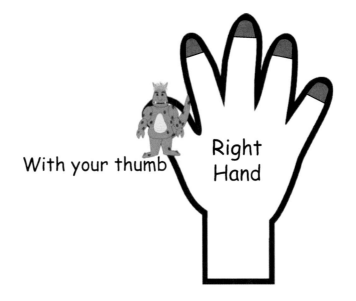

Right Hand

## Play:

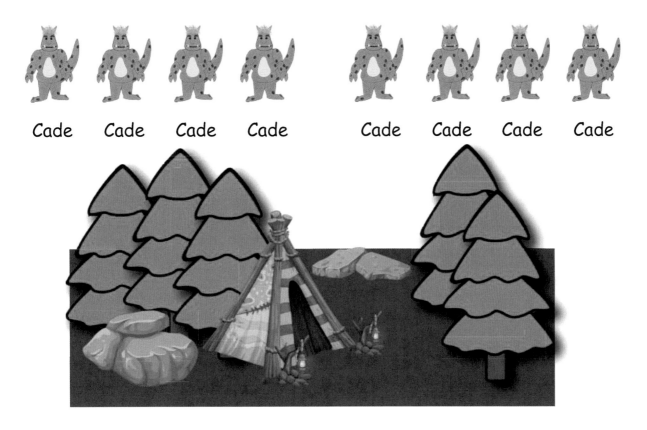

Cade   Cade   Cade   Cade     Cade   Cade   Cade   Cade

# Creature Cade and the Rest

Play:

Cade    Cade    Cade    Rest      Cade    Cade    Cade    Rest

# Rest, Cade, Rest

Play:

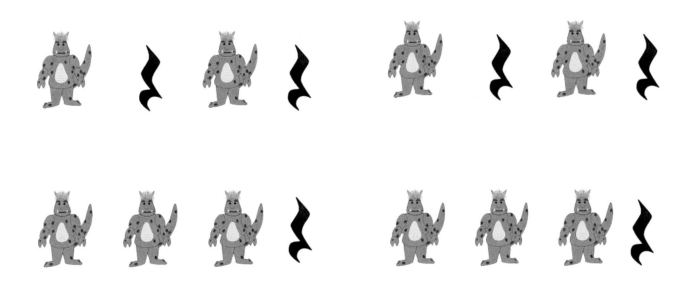

# Cade Loves Orange!

Play:

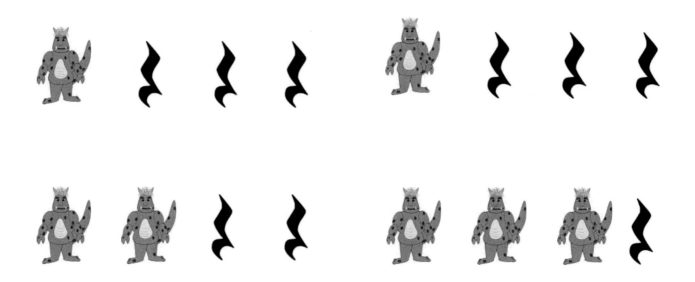

# Let's Be Friends

C D

Right Hand

Play:

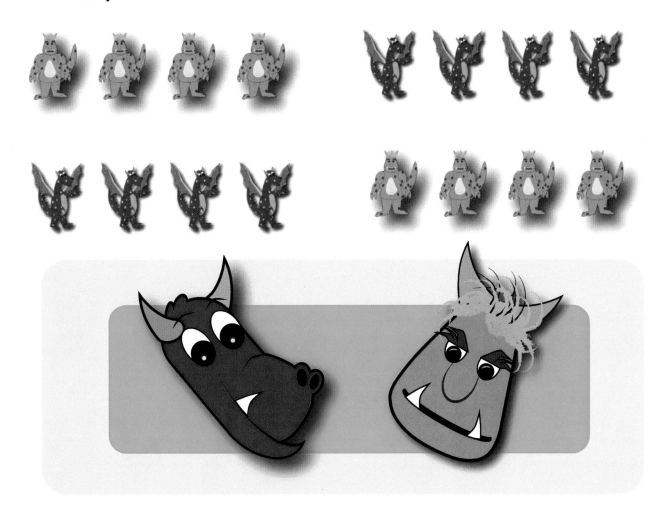

# Cade's Birthday Party

Play:

# Playing Party Games

Play:

# Party Hats

Play:

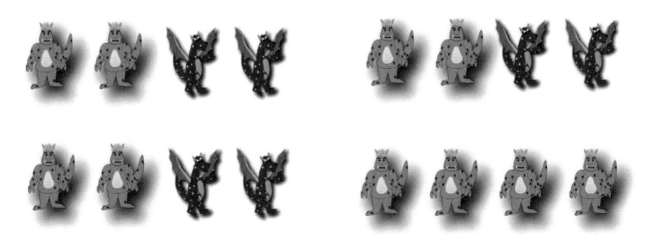

# This is Elix. He is an Eel.
# He is Green.

E

Elix lives on the right side of Dave's cave.

Can you find where Elix lives on the piano?

# Elix the Eel

On this key

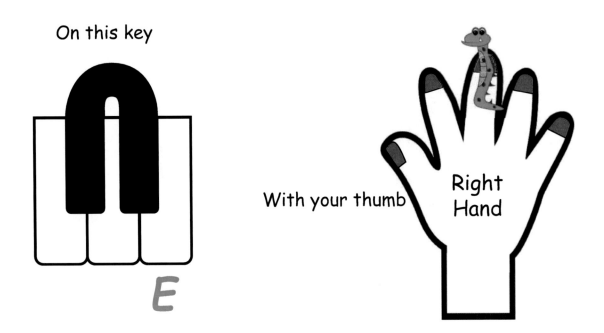

With your thumb

Right Hand

E

## Play:

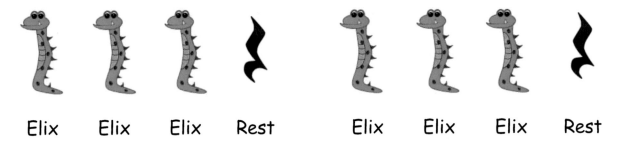

Elix    Elix    Elix    Rest    Elix    Elix    Elix    Rest

# Three Together

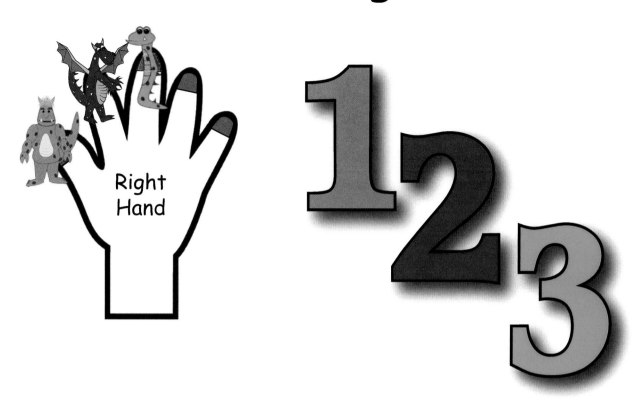

## Play:

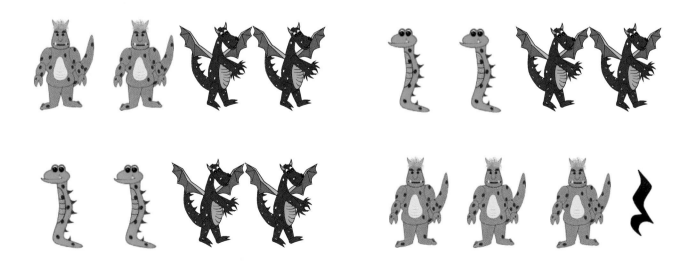

# Up and Down

Play:

# Teeter Totter

Play:

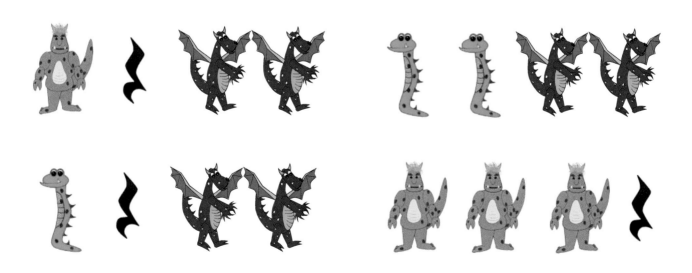

# This is
# Mrs. Treble

She lives on these 5 lines
called a STAFF.

Cade lives on Mrs. Treble by hanging onto her curvy tail.

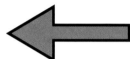

Cade is on the staff, too. He hangs onto this little line just like Mrs. Treble's tail.

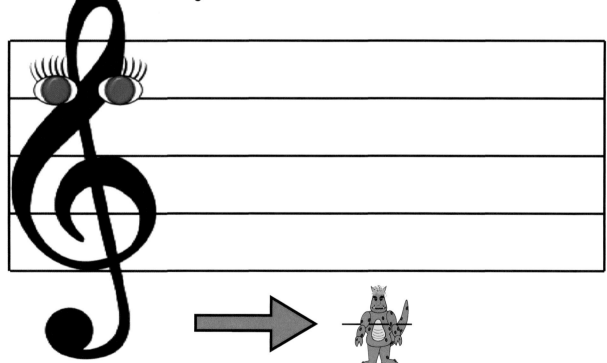

# Play Creature Cade and the Rest while Cade is on the STAFF.

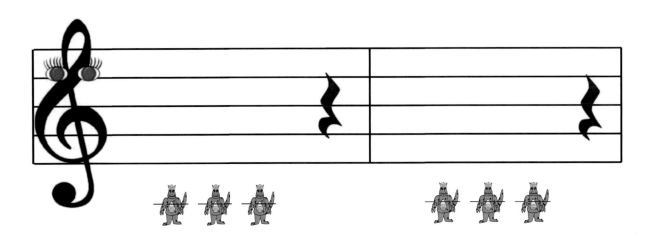

**David** lives on Mrs. Treble by sitting in her curvy tail like a swing.

**Dave** is on the staff, too. He hides underneath the bottom line because it feels like he is in his cave.

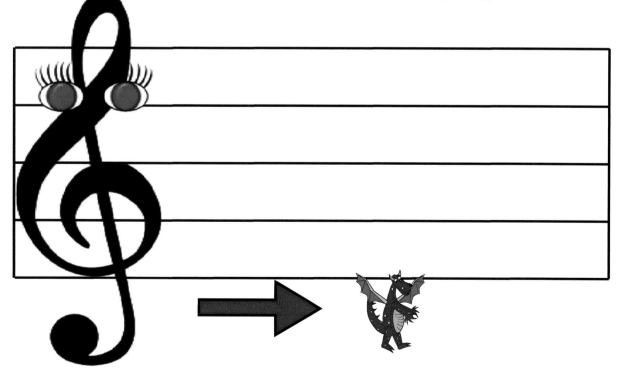

# Play Playing Party Games while
## Cade and Dave are on the STAFF.

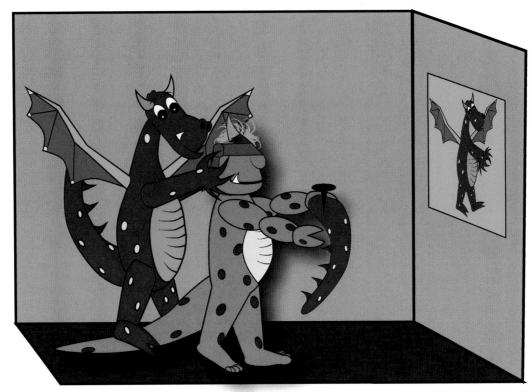

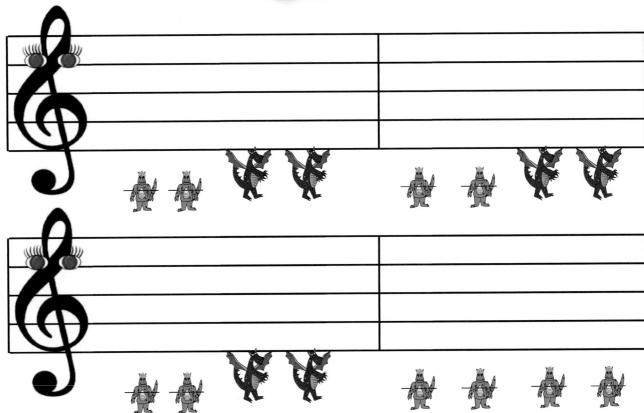

Elix lives on Mrs. Treble by
trying to hide in her
curvy smile.

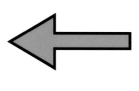

Elix is on the staff, too.
He swims on the bottom line
like it was a river

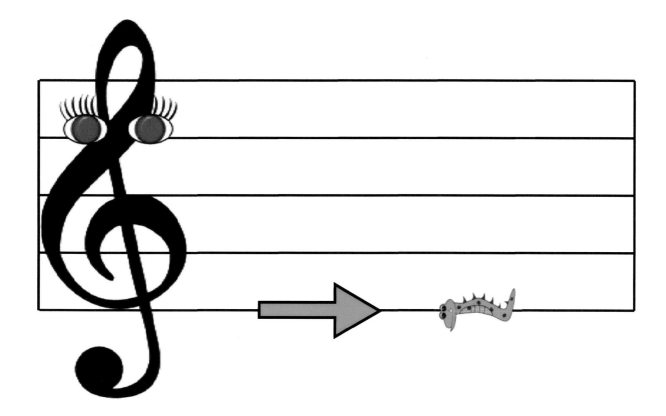

# Play Teeter Totter while
# Cade, Dave and Elix are on the STAFF.

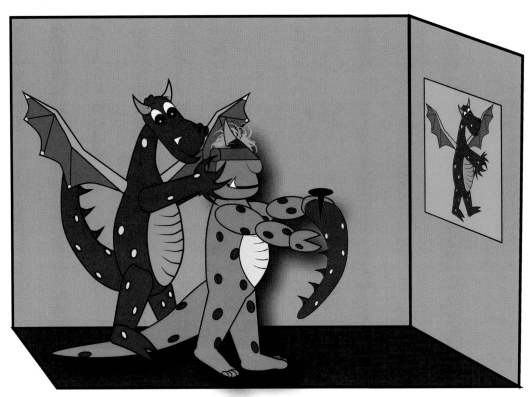

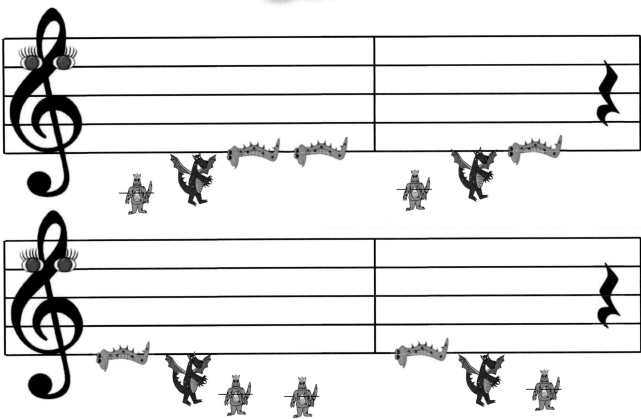

# Magic With Notes

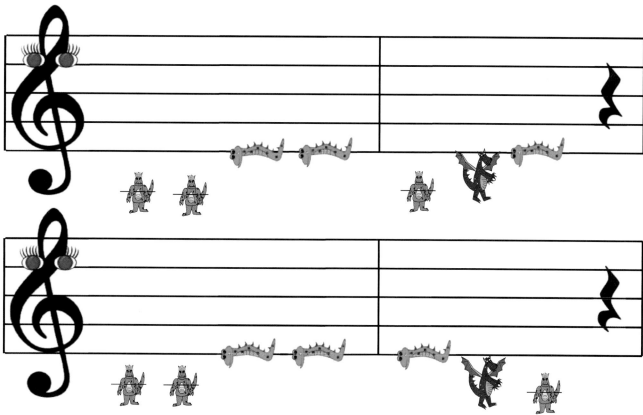

# Magic Drums

# Mary Had A Little Lamb

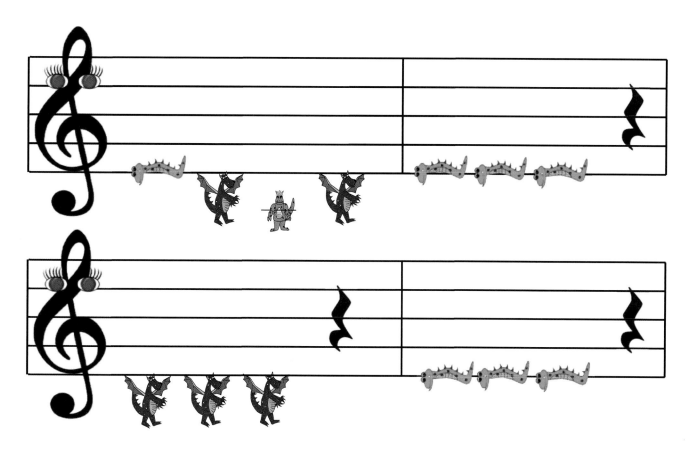

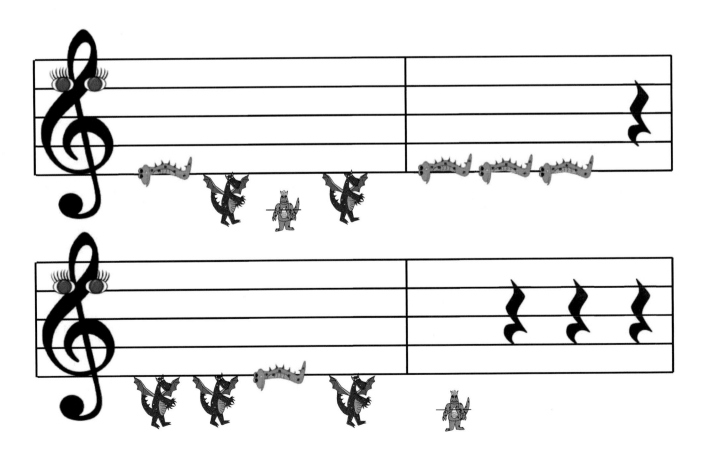

# Going Home

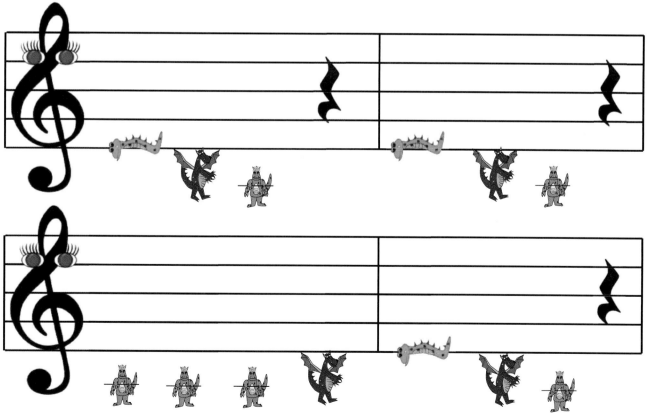

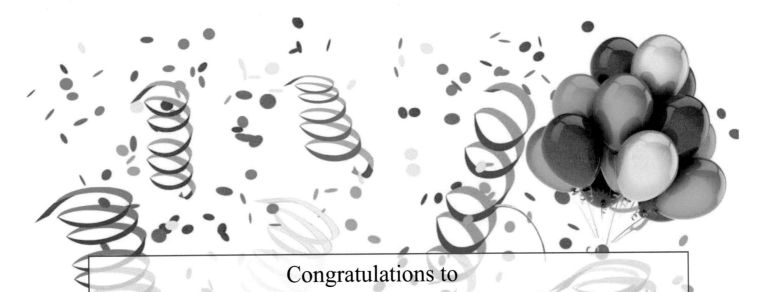

Congratulations to

_____

(Student name)

*for successfully completing*
*Color Me Musical Adagio Piano Book 1*

Made in the USA
Las Vegas, NV
26 February 2023

68207345R00024